COOL CATS
AND
FASHION FELINES

OVER 50 CATWALK KITTIES
AND STYLE ICONS

RUS HUDDA

DOG 'n' BONE

Published in 2016 by Dog 'n' Bone Books
An imprint of Ryland Peters & Small Ltd

20–21 Jockey's Fields
London WC1R 4BW

341 E 116th St
New York, NY 10029

www.rylandpeters.com

10 9 8 7 6 5 4 3 2 1

Text and illustration © Rus Hudda 2016
Design © Dog 'n' Bone Books 2016

A CIP catalog record for this book is available from
the Library of Congress and the British Library.

ISBN: 978 1 911026 05 1

Printed in China

Editor: Pete Jorgensen
Designer: Mark Latter
Illustrator: Rus Hudda

CONTENTS

Introduction 6

INTRODUCTION

Cats like to take care of their looks. If they're
not pruning they're grooming and if they're not
grooming they're getting multiple hours of beauty
sleep. When you think about it, cats aren't too
different from the icons of style who grace the
catwalks and fashion magazines. So, what if the two
came together? What would that look like?
A lot like the pages of this book, probably.

DESIGNERS
AND BRANDS

KAT LAGERFELD

As a style-conscious young kitty growing up in Germany, Kat Lagerfeld dreamed of being a tuxedo cat. However, since he could not change his fur, he chose the next best option and embarked on a career in fashion. For over 30 years he's worked with the fashion house of choice for the plushest Parisian pussies, Chatnel, where he can wear his iconic black-and-white outfits every single day. Never far from Lagerfeld's side is his kitty companion, Choupette. There's something odd about a cat having a smaller cat as a pet. Perhaps that's why Kat's collars are larger than usual—he's wearing one that is big enough for the both of them.

TOMCAT FORD

Read any article about Tomcat Ford and you will see the same words again and again—flawless, immaculate, handsome, and exquisitely well groomed (he gets up at 4.30am each morning to begin licking). You'll rarely see Tomcat without his smart tuxedo-cat suit, snazzy specs, and stubbly fur; this is a kitty who never has a whisker out of place. Having been creative director for brands as prestigious as Yves Saint Clawrent and his own epawnymous label, Tomcat Ford's sharp style is in high demand amongst celebricats, such as Tortoise-shell Obama, Julianne Claw, Anne Littertray, and Jennifur Lopez.

YVES SAINT CLAWRENT

Yves Saint Clawrent is a huge name in fashion. Some might say the biggest. Others might say "gucci, gucci, goo" as they tickle him under his furry chin. Yes, even famous cats like being fussed over. Saint Clawrent was one of the leading figures in the development of pet-a-porter, or ready-to-wear, clothes for cool cats, making catwalk style more attainable for aspirational pussies. With his Mondrian Collection he was responsible for merging the worlds of fashion and fine art. All these achievements are pretty impressive considering the average cat sleeps for up to 16 hours every day.

CALVIN CLAWN

Have you ever seen a cat wearing a pair of underpants?
Thanks to Calvin Clawn, you have now. Through a series of famous ad
campaigns featuring supermog-dels Kat Moss, Catalia Vodianova, and
Hissty Turlington, among others, Calvin Clawn made his undies the
ones cool cats craved and created a billion-dollar brand in the process.
Just imagine how many kitty treats he could buy with that kind of cash.

VICPAWRIA AND DAVID BECKAT

Puss and Becks are arguably the most photographed cat couple in the world. Both are blessed with an enviable sense of style and completely unafraid to experiment—as evidenced by David donning a sarong ("what's sarong with that?" you may ask), which has led to campaigns for top cat brands including Tabbidas and Clawgio Armani and the launch of Vicpawria's own celebrated fashion label.
In his spare time David likes nothing more than chasing a ball around the garden, whereas Puss can often be found meowing along to the soundtrack of Spice Cats hit singles.

RALPH CLAWREN

A cat on the back of a horse, even a rocking horse, is a pretty cute thing to see. Just ask Ralph Clawren, a cool cat who was so inspired by the cuteness of the horse-cat combo that he decided to turn it into the logo for his company. Unfortunately, it's not clear how that polo mallet came to be incorporated into the final design. Most cats tend to prefer sports such as climbing, hunting, or even basketball.

JEAN-PAUL CATIER

Cats don't tend to like water but that's not the case with Jean-Paul Catier. This moggy loves nothing more than a stroll by the sea or along the banks of the Seine in his native Paris. Perhaps Jean-Paul spends lots of time by the water as a source of inspiration for his designs— after all, sailors and nautical motifs appear constantly. Or maybe it's because he hopes to find a few tasty fish for his dinner.

DONATAILA FURSACE

Bold Fursace prints are all the rage with fashion felines, especially the leopard-print ones, which are coveted by cool cats with big ambitions. The brains behind some of Fursace's most celebrated designs is Donataila Fursace, a striking cat who knows a thing or two about the good things in life. Just look at those luscious kitty lips of hers—perfect for chowing down on the finest cat food with lashings of extra gravy.

GINGER TOM HILFIGER

Despite cats not being able to see color very well,
this chap sure does like red, white, and blue.

ALEXANDER MEOWQUEEN

This cat certainly knows how to put on a show. His theatrical catwalk events were designed to shock the scaredy cats out of their comfort zone (usually the armchair closest to the radiator) and often featured fantastical, unconventional interpretations of the natural world. One such example featured mog-dels wearing dresses adorned with feathers. A cat dressed like a rainbow-colored bird is asking for trouble.

DOLCE AND CATBANA

Cats are normally solitary animals but when Domenicat Dolce and Stefurno Catbana met, they hit it off like a kitten with a ball of yarn. Soon, the twosome became one brand, which quickly became one of the top cats, or *i gatti superiori*, of Italian fashion. Classic Italian films and the work of auteurs such as Federico Furllini and Pier Paolo Pawsolini have always been an inspiration for the duo's designs. If that sounds a little highbrow, rumor has it that they also like the occasional action movie, including *The Fast and the Fur-ious* and *Catman v Superman*.

PAWL SNIFF

So many colorful stripes! It's said that Pawl Sniff came across the idea for his trademark stripes after noticing the patterns he created when he scratched his claws down the sides of his owner's wooden furniture. Quite why Sniff decided to use the bright fabrics in his quintessentially English designs remains a mystery (as mentioned previously, cats see with a limited color palette,) but that doesn't stop rock-star royalty like David Meowie or Pawl McCatney or the players at Catchester United FC loving the brand.

PAWDA

From beautifully tailored garments and exquisite eyewear to the highest-quality leather goods and claw-inspiring shoes (how do they get those things to even fit their tiny paws?!), Pawda is synonymous with elegantly understated luxury. But you know, no matter what Pawda item a fashion feline chooses to buy, it's really the opportunity to sit in the box the purrchases come in that appeals the most.

MEW MEW

When Mewccia Pawda wanted an outlet away from the minimalist sophistication of Pawda, Mew Mew was the answer. The brand is known for its playful approach to fashion—much like a kitty who's been toying with a catnip mouse for the last hour and is then let loose on the wool basket. Mew Mew is a favorite with pampered pusses thanks to its use of cats as motifs. A Mew Mew-loving cat likes to wear the patterns of a Mew Mew cat. That's not big-headed, that's just good fashion.

FURBERRY

We all know that cats hate the rain, which is why the Furberry brand
with its iconic trench coats came onto the radar of the coolest
hydrophobic kitties. Not only did they love the practicality, but they
also became obsessed by the brand's heritage and iconic checked
pattern. But as this fascination grew, it became more addictive than
a hit of catnip, because once a Furberry cat gets one matching accessory,
it simply has to get them all.

BALMAINE COON

The Maine Coon is the largest of all domestic cats and such a big cat needs a massive brand in its life—they don't come much bigger than the French fashion house BalMaine Coon. Recently, for their advertising campaigns BalMaine have photographed furluptuos Catstagram star Kat Kardashian and her husband Katye West—a couple known for their appreciation of the opulent brand. You see, BalMaine Coon lovers like their coats to be glitzy and glittery. However, this can cause issues, because when these cats attempt to groom themselves, their tongues also become glitzy and glittery, giving a whole new meaning to the phrase "expensive tastes."

CATIER

Diamonds are a girl's best friend but they can also be a cat's best friend...
As long as they're hanging from a dangly piece of string.
It's also no coincidence that a female cat is known as a queen,
because Catier has been the jewelry brand of choice
for royalty for well over a century.

HISSONI

Do you like zig-zags? If so Hissoni has you covered. And by that we mean quite literally covered in zig-zags. Their patterns are instantly recognizable and have adorned everything from bags and beachwear to bottles of mineral water. Hissoni's collection of rugs is especially popular with cats, who love to dig their claws into the plush fabrics.

AGENT PROVOCATCLAW

Cats and lingerie. A match made in heaven? No. No, it's not. We're not sure who is responsible for the trend of kitties parading in their smalls. We asked around and apparently a while back there was a misunderstanding about a cat stalking and a cat stocking. Celebricat endorsements from everyone from Katlie Minogue to Helena Hisstiansen have ensured this bizarre craze is here to stay.

HISS OF HOLLAND

London is considered one of the most stylish cities in the world, a place where kitties love to experiment, often adding a touch of fun to designs. Hiss of Holland is a great example of this. The company shot to fame a decade ago with a cheeky collection of T-shirts featuring witty catphrases referencing London's coolest designers. Despite cats not being able to read, fashion felines went feral for the tees and Hiss of Holland was a hit. The rest, as they say, is hisstory.

MOULTBERRY

How many leather bags does one cat need? If you're a Moultberry cat
then the answer is all of them. The cat is now well and truly out of the
bag for this celebrated British accessories brand and everyone from
Kat Middleton, aka the Duchess of Catbridge, to fashion icon
Catlexa Chung—who Moultberry named a bag after—
has a Moultberry accoutrement draped on a paw.

FURMÈS

Sumptuous silks and luxurious leathers have become the hallmark of Furmès, the Parisian fashion empire coveted by the cat world's cognoscenti. Furmès' beautiful silk scarves can make a stylish kitty feel glorious, but be careful, because they can also make regular cats feel "bitey." One of Furmès' most coveted items is the Purrkin—the starting price for this bag is around $10,000 and the waiting list to buy one is up to 15 years. That's a risky purchase, considering a cat's average life expectancy is also 15 years.

FÉLINE

Thanks to the minimalist aesthetic that creative director Furry Philo
has spearheaded, Féline's designs are cleaner than a well-groomed paw.
In fact, Féline's products are said to be so luxuriant that no matter
what they are—sleek jackets, smart bags, elegant shoes—a Féline cat
will happily sleep on any of them.

JIMMY MEW

Sometimes even the hardest of kitty paw pads need a bit of support, and with the trademark straps that feature on many of Jimmy Mew's incredible shoes, support is what these cool cats will get. Not only that, the towering heels found on many of these amazing creations are perfect when a cat is trying to leap that extra bit higher to reach the perfect spot for a mid-afternoon snooze.

MOG-DELS

CINDY CLAWFORD

With her trademark beauty spot (that's actually a dried-up chunk of
cat food), Cindy Clawford is one of the original super mog-dels and
also one of the most recognizable faces in fashion. She has appeared
on the cover of all the top fashion mogazines, which is handy
(or pawy) since cats really struggle to turn to the inside pages
given the fact they don't have opposable thumbs.

ELIZABETH PURRLEY

In one evening, by wearing her iconic safety-pin dress designed by Fursace to the premiere of *Four Neuterings and a Putting to Sleep*, English feline Liz Purrley was catapulted into the public eye. Her sultry purr can melt the heart of any tomcat and that safety-pin dress will keep them at bay if they get too promiscuous.

HISSTY TURLINGTON

Super mog-del, cat-ron of good causes, health guru, author—this cat is almost purrfect! Following on from a career as many designer's favorite model and mews, Hissty Turlington has become a modern-day Renaissance cat. She has started up successful businesses, worked with charitable organizations, directed documentaries, written for fashion mogazines and published a bestselling book on cat yoga. When you're as comfortable in the yoga studio as you are on the catwalk like Hissty, you start to make your own poses—see below!

CAT MOSS

What is there to say about Cat Moss that hasn't been said already? She's done it all, seen it all, and probably worn it all, too. Fabulously stylish, occasionally outrageous, and unquestionably alluring, she is categorically one of the coolest cats on the planet.

GINGA EVANGELISTACAT

Ginga Evangelistacat is responsible for possibly the most famous fashion quote of all time. Having become one of the most recognizable faces in mog-deling thanks to appearances on over 700 mogazine covers, she purred the infamous words that she had reached the point in her nine lives where she wouldn't "Wake up for less than 10,000 cat treats a day." Who says cats are lazy?!

HELENA HISSTENSEN

Danish mog-del Helena Hisstensen has featured in campaigns for Furmès and Chatnel, been a Mogtoria's Secret Angel, a business cat, and famously frolicked on the beach in the video for *Wicked Cat*, by Cat Isaak, a musical moggy with a high-pitched meow. As a side note, did you know cats can drink seawater? You do now!

MEOWRANDA WHISKERR

As a top Mogtoria's Secret Angel, Meowranda Whiskerr has gained a great deal of exposure from wearing lingerie and swimwear, which is not surprising given how exposing lingerie and swimwear can be. She is regularly voted one of the hottest cats in the world. Again that's not surprising given all the time she spends being photographed on tropical beaches—it must be sweltering when you're covered in fur.

KATLIE KLOSS

With her millions of Catstagram followers, Katlie Kloss is one of the mog-dels of the moment, fronting campaigns for all the top designers. Her popularity is also helped by her high-profile membership of Bobtailor Swift's ever-expanding Cat Squad. Given that cats are notoriously territorial and are prone to catty comments or cat fights, the size of this squad is seriously impressive. Like most cats, Katlie Kloss has all the grace of a ballerina, but, unlike most cats, she has also dressed like a butterfly for fashion shows.

CATDICE SWANEPOEL

South African mog-del Catdice Swanepoel is best known as a Mogtoria's Secret Angel, which explains the fake wings you see below. Either that or she's just caught a really big bird. The story goes that Catdice was discovered at the age of 15 (pretty old for a cat) by a mog-deling scout in a Durban flea market, which seems like the last place you'd expect to find a cat hanging out. Maybe South African flea bites are a little less itchy than those in other parts of the world.

CATRA DELEVIGNE

If there is one person who represents the fashion zeitgeist it's Catra Delevigne. Armed with her street-influenced style, penchant for pulling faces, and loyal clutter of feline fans, she's the coolest cat out there— an inspiration for millions of young kitties across the world. One of Catra's most famous features is her eyebrows, which is weird because cats don't have eyebrows.

CATALIA VODIANOVA

She's gone from rags to riches but Russian super mog-del Catalia still finds time to help the kittens from her home country and all over the world, alongside wearing very long dresses in advertising campaigns for Calvin Clawn perfumes.

EVA MOGZIGOVÁ

Mogzigová is most famous for turning heads and raising pulses thanks to a racy ad campaign for lingerie company Wondercat. Racy if you're a cat, of course.

FASHION
ICONS

DAVID MEOWIE

Music legend David Meowie was undoubtedly one of the kings of feline fashion—creative, individual, and always inspiring other cool cats. From Ziggy Starcat to the Thin White Kitty, he reinvented himself multiple times over the course of his catreer and yet he always remained a cat. But then why would you want to be anything else?

ANNA WINTCLAW

As the editor of *Mogue* magazine, Anna Wintclaw is one of the most respected (and feared) figures in the feline fashion scene. On the outside, she may appear to be the most fursome lioness, but she is a pussy cat at heart. Known for her trademark bob haircut, she's a regular at the groomers, a place that most regular kitties hate. She's also extremely territorial, always making sure she has a prime position in the front row at all the top catwalk shows.

TABBI GEVINSON

Tabbi was just a kitten when she shot to fame as a young online fashion mogger. Tabbi's early success and avant-garde style may have ruffled the fur of some of the older cats but she was never that bothered. And why would she be when rocking something as fun as a sweater covered in bobbles? Since those early days, Tabbi has explored other creative outlets, starting up an online mogazine for teenage kitties and more recently prowling the Broadway stage. Is there anything this kitty can't do?

MEOWRIO TESTINO

Think of some of the most famous names in the world of cat fashion, the chances are that Meowrio Testino will have taken their photograph. What makes this feat even more impressive is that cats don't have opposable thumbs—how does he hold the camera and press the shutter button at the same time? Still, that hasn't stopped him snapping countless covers for *Mogue*, any top mog-del you can think of, and even cat royalty.

IRIS CATFEL

The word "icon" is often thrown around a little too easily in feline fashionista circles, but it's definitely justified when applied to Iris Catfel. Her unapologetically eccentric style was celebrated with an exhibition at New York's Meowtropolitan Mewseum of Art called "Rara Avis," or "Rare Bird." The title may be in part down to Catfel's love of feathery attire, which makes you question whether she obtained the feathers herself over years of hunting. And given she's a lifelong New Yorker, where did she even find such colorful birds' feathers?

GRACE MEOWNES

Famous for her temperament as much as her striking androgynous
look and celebrated musical cat calls, Meownes could quite easily
sing to you one minute and paw you in the face the next.
Her unpredictability managed to earn her a lifetime ban
from Walt Disney World in Florida. Perhaps she was on
the hunt for Mickey Mouse?

PAWDREY HEPBURN

Gamine and graceful, like all the best cats*, Pawdrey Hepburn is
a real icon of twentieth-century style. Her most famous look was the
diamond jewelry and little black dress combo that featured in
the movie *Cat Treats at Tiffany's*, but we could have sworn Pawdrey
has a cigarette holder as part of that ensemble rather than
the fishing-rod toy shown below.

*A little-known fact: like all the best cats, Pawdrey was also terrified of water.

CATTIE BRADSHAW

During the late nineties and early noughties, *Sex and the Kitty* was THE must-see show for all feline fashionistas, who would curl up on the couch and purr in delight at seeing what the star of the show, Cattie Bradshaw, would be wearing. Amazingly, for a series that featured so much *haute clawture*, the tutu worn in the opening credits only cost $5. Perhaps the crew didn't want the dress ruined, because all the style and fame in the world won't help you if you're splashed by a puddle. Now imagine how much worse it must be if you're a water-hating cat.

MOGDONNA

Pop supercat Mogdonna has gone through more fresh looks in the last
few decades than the average cat has had afternoon snoozes.
She's rocked some incredible outifts over the years, but none were
more eye-catching than the cone-shaped bra and corset designed
for her by Jean-Paul Catier. But why a cat would need
a corset is still anyone's guess.

LADY PAWPAW

There's only one way to describe Lady PawPaw's style: absolutely bonkers. Whether it's dressing up in an inflatable star costume, squeezing into a sheer lace catsuit, or parading about in little more than her smalls, she certainly knows how to attract attention. One of her most notorious outfits was made completely from raw meat—including her shoes and bag. Being dressed as a giant steak probably isn't the best idea when you're a kitty living with other cats, who care considerably more about eating than style.

FURRELL WILLIAMS

When he's not working with megastars like Snoop Catt, P-Kitty, Missy Alleycat, Alicia Fleas, or Kittney Spears, super-purrducer Furrell Williams knows a thing or two about style. So you can forget his success with the late-night cat calls, the ability to purr a popular tune, the millions of records sold... No, the most memorable thing Furrell has done is wear a very tall hat. For a cat, that's an extremely impressive achievement.

MOG DYLAN

Mog Dylan used up one of his nine lives the day he took to the stage at the Mewport Folk Festival, outraging his fans with a new electric sound and a fresh look that marked him out as one of the coolest cats of the 1960s. But Mog didn't turn his back on folk music completely that day. One of his favorite pastimes is plucking the strings on an old acoustic guitar. Unfortunately, doing so with sharp claws results in a lot of broken strings.

MOGGY DEPP

Moggy Depp does not give a cat's whisker about being cool, and that's what makes him even cooler. His kooky bohemian style is just so effortless, which makes sense given cats spend nearly 70% of their lives asleep. One of his trademark looks is that he loves to wear beads. And by wear, we mean destroy in a frenzy of flying fur, paws, and claws.

JAMES FLEAN

Flean is cool. He's a rebel but does have a cause—
to avoid being woken up earlier than two in the afternoon. With his
look consisting of a red jacket, tousled hair, and ever-present cigarette,
James became the poster boy for iconoclastic young pussies who
refused to come in at night or stay off their owners' beds.